The Everyday Italian Cookbook

Simple Italian Dishes for Everyday Meals

BY

Carla Hale

License Notes

No part of this Book can be reproduced in any form or by any means including print, electronic, scanning or photocopying unless prior permission is granted by the author.

All ideas, suggestions and guidelines mentioned here are written for informative purposes. While the author has taken every possible step to ensure accuracy, all readers are advised to follow information at their own risk. The author cannot be held responsible for personal and/or commercial damages in case of misinterpreting and misunderstanding any part of this Book

Table of Contents

Introduction

Every year in Italy, there are thousands of tourists that travels from all over the world not only to see the country from themselves, but to enjoy the cuisine as well. Italian cuisine is steeped in a rich tradition that it is envied throughout the world. However, most visitors to the country believe that the only dishes served in Italy are pizza and tiramisu. While these dishes are essential staples, the country is more than just these popular dishes.

If you have always wanted to learn how to prepare authentic Italian cuisine from the comfort of your own home, then this is one Italian cookbook you need to check out for yourself. By the end of this book, not only will you discover some of the most authentic Italian dishes you will ever find, but you will also learn how to prepare them correctly.

So, let's stop wasting time and get to cooking!

Sausage and Broccoli Rabe Frittata

To kick things off in this Italian cookbook, we have an Italian breakfast that I know you will want to make every morning.

Makes: 8 servings

Total Prep Time: 35 minutes

Ingredients:

- 12 eggs, beaten
- ½ cup of whole milk
- ¾ cup of cheddar cheese, grated and evenly divided
- Dash of salt and black pepper
- 2 Tbsp. of vegetable oil
- ½ of an onion, chopped
- ½ pound of Spanish chorizo, casing removed
- 1 bunch of broccoli rabe, chopped

Directions:

1. Preheat the oven to broil.

2. In a bowl, add in the beaten eggs and whole milk. Add in ½ cup of grated cheddar cheese. Whisk until lightly beaten. Season with a dash of salt and black pepper.

3. In a skillet set over medium to high heat, add in the vegetable oil. Add in the chopped onion and Spanish chorizo. Cook for 8 to 10 minutes or until the chorizo is browned.

4. Add in the broccoli rabe. Season again with a dash of salt and black pepper. Cook for 8 to 10 minutes.

5. Lower the heat to low. Pour the eggs over the veggies. Continue to cook for 10 to 12 minutes.

6. Top off with the remaining grated cheddar cheese.

7. Place into the oven to broil for 5 minutes or until golden brown.

8. Remove. Slice into wedges and serve.

Skillet Ravioli Lasagna

This is a delicious Italian dish that incorporates the flavor of both ravioli and lasagna, to make a dish that every Italian food lover will love.

Makes: 4 servings

Total Prep Time: 30 minutes

Ingredients:

- 1 pound of hot Italian sausage, casings
- 2 cups of marinara sauce
- ½ cup of water
- 1 pound of cheese ravioli
- 1 ½ cup of ricotta cheese
- 1 egg
- Dash of salt and black pepper
- 1 cup of mozzarella cheese, shredded

Directions:

1. Preheat the oven to broil.

2. In a cast iron skillet set over a high medium to high heat, add in the sausage. Cook for 8 to 10 minutes until browned. Drain the excess fat.

3. Add in the marinara sauce and water. Stir well to mix. Allow to come to a simmer.

4. Add in the cheese ravioli and cook for 10 minutes or until the sauce is thick in consistency.

5. In a bowl, add in the ricotta cheese and egg. Season with a dash of salt and black pepper. Stir well to mix. Drop this mix by the spoonful into the skillet. Cook for 3 minutes.

6. Sprinkle the shredded mozzarella cheese over the top.

7. Transfer the skillet into the oven to broil for 3 minutes or until gold.

8. Remove and set aside to cool for 10 minutes before serving.

Easy Eggplant Parmesan

While this delicious Italian dish may cause an oozy mess with practically every bite, it is so delicious, I know you won't be able to get enough of it.

Makes: 12 servings

Total Prep Time: 3 hours and 45 minutes

Ingredients for the marinara:

- ¼ cup of extra virgin olive oil
- 1 head of garlic, crushed
- 1 red onion, chopped
- 3 anchovy fillets, packed in oil and optional
- ½ tsp. of crushed red pepper flakes
- 1 Tbsp. of tomato paste
- ¼ cup of dried white wine
- 2, 28 ounce cans of tomatoes, whole and peeled
- ¼ cup of basil leaves, torn
- ½ tsp. of oregano
- Dash of salt

Ingredients for the eggplant:

- 4 pounds of Italian eggplants, peeled and thinly sliced
- Dash of salt
- 3 cup of panko breadcrumbs
- 1 ½ tsp. of oregano
- 1 tsp. of black pepper
- 1 ½ cups of Parmesan cheese, grated and evenly divided
- 1 ½ cups of white flour
- 5 eggs, beaten

- 1 1/3 cups of extra virgin olive oil
- ½ cup of basil and parsley, chopped and extra for serving
- 6 ounces of mozzarella cheese, grated
- 8 ounces of mozzarella, thinly sliced

Directions:

1. Prepare the marinara. Preheat the oven to 350 degrees.

2. In a pot set over medium to high heat, add in the extra virgin olive oil. Add in the crushed garlic and cook for 5 minutes or until gold. Add in the chopped red onion and crushed red pepper flakes. Stir to mix and continue to cook for another 5 minutes or until the onion is translucent.

3. Add in the tomato paste. Cook for 2 minutes.

4. Add in the dried white wine and allow to come to a boil. Cook for 1 minute or until evaporated. Add in the tomatoes, dried basil and oregano. Stir well to mix.

5. Add in 1 ½ cups of water and stir well to incorporate. Season with a dash of salt and black pepper.

6. Transfer the pot into the oven. Cook for 2 to 2 ½ hours. Remove and set aside to cool. Transfer into a food processor. Pulse on the highest setting until smooth in consistency.

7. Prepare the eggplant. Season the eggplant slices with a dash of salt. Cover with paper towels and place onto a baking sheet. Weigh down with a pot. Set aside for 45 minutes to 1 hour.

8. In a food processor, add in the panko breadcrumbs, oregano, ¾ cup of the Parmesan cheese and a dash of black pepper. Pulse until finely ground. Transfer this mix into a bowl.

9. Preheat the oven to 350 degrees.

10. In a bowl, add in flour. In a separate bowl add in the eggs. Dredge the eggplant slices into the flour, coating on all sides. Dip into the egg and roll in the panko breadcrumbs. Place onto a wire rack.

11. In a skillet set over medium to high heat, add in 2/3 cup of the vegetable oil. Add in the eggplant slices. Cook for 5 minutes or until gold. Transfer onto a plate lined with paper towels to drain. Season with a dash of salt.

12. In a bowl, add in the chopped basil and parsley, grated mozzarella cheese and remaining ¾ cup of parmesan cheese. Stir well to mix.

13. Spread 1 cup of the marinara sauce into a baking dish. Add the eggplant slices. Drizzle another cup of the marinara sauce over the eggplant slices. Add 1/3 of the cheese mix. Repeat the layers 2 more times, making sure to top off with the cheese mix. Cover with a sheet of aluminum foil.

14. Place into the oven to bake for 45 minutes to 1 hour.

15. Remove and place the fresh mozzarella cheese slices over the eggplant.

16. Increase the temperature of the oven to 425 degrees. Continue to bake for 15 to 20 minutes.

17. Remove and set aside to rest for 30 minutes before serving.

Radicchio and Olive Panzanella

Make this delicious dish as an appetizer to your next Italian dinner night. Make sure to serve with freshly baked bread for the tastiest results.

Makes: 4 servings

Total Prep Time: 15 minutes

Ingredients:

- 6 ounces of country bread, torn into pieces
- 1 Tbsp. of lemon zest, grated
- ½ cup of extra virgin olive oil, evenly divided
- Dash of salt and black pepper
- 1 shallot, chopped
- 2 Tbsp. of lemon juice
- 2 Tbsp. of red wine vinegar
- 1 Tbsp. of oregano, chopped
- 1 head of radicchio, torn into pieces
- 1 fennel bulb, thinly sliced
- 1 cup of flat leaf parsley, chopped
- ½ cup of green olives, pitted and cut into halves
- 3 ounces of sheep's milk cheese, shaved
- 3 ounces of salami, thinly sliced

Directions:

1. Preheat the oven to 400 degrees.

2. On a baking sheet, add the bread, fresh lemon zest and ¼ cup of the olive oil. Toss well until coated. Season with a dash of salt and black pepper.

3. Place into the oven to bake for 8 to 10 minutes. Remove and set aside to cool.

4. In a bowl, add in the chopped shallot, lemon juice, red wine vinegar and chopped oregano. Stir well to mix. Season with a dash of salt and black pepper. Add in ¼ cup of the olive oil and whisk to mix.

5. In the bowl, add in the radicchio, sliced fennel bulb, green olive halves, shaved cheese, sliced salami and bread pieces. Toss well until coated.

6. Serve immediately.

Easy Tomato and Butter Spaghetti

This is a delicious Italian dish you can make whenever you need something easy to make after a long day at the office. It is so easy to make, it can be made in just a matter of minutes.

Makes: 4 servings

Total Prep Time: 25 minutes

Ingredients:

- 1 Tbsp. of extra virgin olive oil
- 1 onion, chopped
- Dash of salt and black pepper
- 2 cloves of garlic, minced
- 3 pound of tomatoes, chopped
- 1 Tbsp. of dried oregano
- 4 Tbsp. of butter, soft
- 8 ounces of spaghetti, cooked
- ¼ cup of basil leaves, torn
- Parmesan cheese, grated and for serving

Directions:

1. In a skillet set over medium to high heat, add in the olive oil. Add in the chopped onion. Season with a dash of salt and black pepper. Cook for 5 minutes or until soft.

2. Add in the chopped tomatoes and stir well to mix. Continue to cook for another 3 to 5 minutes.

3. Allow to come to a simmer. Lower the heat to low. Add in the butter. Season with a dash of salt and black pepper. Add in the oregano. Stir well to mix. Continue to simmer for 15 minutes. Remove from heat.

4. Pour the sauce over the cooked spaghetti.

5. Serve with a topping of the torn basil and grated Parmesan cheese.

Pasta e Fagioli

This is a classic Italian dish that you will be able to make with complete ease. Made with aromatic and classic Italian flavors, this is a dish that won't fail to disappoint.

Makes: 4 servings

Total Prep Time: 3 hours

Ingredients:

- 1 ½ cups of dried cannellini beans, soaked
- 2 ounces of parmesan rind
- Parmesan cheese, shaved and for serving
- 2 carrots, cut into halves
- 2 stalks of celery, sliced into halves
- 1 head of garlic, chopped
- 6 sprigs of parsley, chopped
- 1 sprig of rosemary, chopped
- 2 bay leaves
- 2 dried chiles de arbol, crushed and extra for serving
- Dash of salt and black pepper
- 3 Tbsp. of extra virgin olive oil
- 1 onion, chopped
- 1, 14.5 ounce can of tomatoes, peeled and whole
- ¾ cup of dried white wine
- 3 ounces of dried lasagna
- ½ of a head of escarole, torn into pieces

Directions:

1. In a pot set over medium to high heat, add in the soaked cannellini beans, parmesan rind, carrot halves, celery halves, garlic, chopped parsley, chopped rosemary, bay leaves, crushed chiles de arbol and 2 quarts of water. Stir well to mix.

2. Allow to come to a boil. Lower the heat to low. Cook for 1 ½ hours or until soft. Season with a dash of salt and black pepper. Remove from heat and set aside to cool for 30 minutes.

3. Toss out the vegetables, parmesan rind and bay leaves.

4. In a pot set over medium to high heat, add in 3 tablespoons of olive oil. Add in the chopped onion and garlic. Cook for 8 to 10 minutes or until soft.

5. Add in the tomatoes and continue to cook for 10 to 15 minutes. Add in the white wine. Allow to come to a boil. Boil for 5 minutes or until evaporated.

6. Add in the beans and liquid. Cook for 10 to 15 minutes.

7. Add in the lasagna and cook for 20 minutes or until soft.

8. Add in the escarole and continue to cook for an additional minute. Season with a dash of salt and black pepper.

9. Remove from heat.

10. Serve with a drizzling of oil and grated Parmesan cheese over the top.

Caprese Stuffed Shells

This is a delicious stuffed shell recipe you can prepare whenever you are craving homemade Italian food. Once you get a taste of it, you will feel as if you are sitting right in the heart of Italy.

Makes: 4 servings

Total Prep Time: 40 minutes

Ingredients:

- 15 jump pasta shells
- 2 cups of ricotta cheese
- 1 cup of mozzarella cheese, shredded
- ¾ cup of sun dried tomatoes, chopped and evenly divided
- 2 Tbsp. of basil, chopped
- Dash of salt and black pepper
- ½ cup of low sodium chicken broth
- ½ cup of heavy whipping cream

Directions:

1. Preheat the oven to 350 degrees.

2. In a pot set over medium to high heat, fill with salted water. Add in the pasta shells. Cook for 8 to 10 minutes or until soft. Drain and set the shells aside to cool.

3. In a bowl, add in the ricotta cheese, shredded mozzarella cheese, half of the tomatoes and chopped basil. Season with a dash of salt and black pepper. Stir well to evenly mix.

4. In a saucepan set over low heat, add in the low sodium chicken broth, heavy whipping cream and remaining tomatoes. Stir well to mix and allow to come to a simmer. Cook for 5 minutes.

5. Pour ¾ of the sauce into a baking dish.

6. Spoon the filling into the pasta shells. Place the shells into the baking dish. Pour the remaining ¼ of the sauce over the top.

7. Place into the oven to bake for 15 to 20 minutes.

8. Remove and serve immediately.

Italian Vegetable Stew

Make this perfect Italian dish whenever you are feeling under the weather. One bite and I guarantee you will begin feeling better in no time.

Makes: 6 to 8 servings

Total Prep Time: 3 hours and 20 minutes

Ingredients:

- ½, 1 pound loaf of sourdough bread, torn into pieces
- 1 bunch of collard greens
- 1 bunch of Tuscan kale, chopped
- Dash of salt
- ½ cup of olive oil, evenly divided and extra for serving
- 2 carrots, chopped
- 2 stalks of celery, chopped
- 1 leek, chopped
- 4 cloves of garlic, chopped
- ½ tsp. of red pepper flakes
- 1, 28 ounce can of tomatoes, whole, peeled and drained
- 8 cups of low sodium vegetable broth
- 3, 15 ounce cans of cannellini beans, rinsed
- 4 sprigs of thyme
- 1 sprig of marjoram
- 1 bay leaf
- Dash of black pepper
- Parmesan cheese, shaved and for serving

Directions:

1. Place the bread pieces onto a baking sheet. Set aside to dry out for 2 hours.

2. In a pot set over medium to high heat, fill with salted water. Add in the collard greens and kale. Cook for 3 minutes or until soft. Remove and rinse under running water. Chop and set aside.

3. In a pot set over medium to high heat, add in ¼ cup of extra virgin olive oil. Add in the chopped carrots, chopped celery and chopped leek. Stir well to mix. Cook for 8 to 10 minutes or until soft.

4. Add in the chopped garlic and crushed red pepper flakes. Stir well to mix. Continue to cook for an additional minute.

5. Add in the tomatoes and crush finely. Continue to cook for 15 minutes.

6. Add in the vegetable broth, rinsed cannellini beans, thyme sprigs, bay leaf and cooked kale and collard greens. Season with a dash of salt and black pepper. Allow to come to a boil. Lower the heat to low. Cook for 40 to 50 minutes.

7. Remove the bay leaves. Serve immediately.

Italian Tiramisu

If you are looking for a classic Italian dessert dish to serve to your family, then this is the perfect dish for you to make. It is so tasty, it will satisfy any strong sweet tooth.

Makes: 8 servings

Total Prep Time: 20 minutes

Ingredients for the sponge cake:

- 4 eggs, separated
- 1 cup of white sugar, evenly divided
- ½ cup of white flour
- ¼ cup of cornstarch
- Dash of salt

Ingredients for the mascarpone cream:

- 2 cups of mascarpone
- ½ cup of white sugar
- 4 egg yolks
- 2 Tbsp. of dark rum
- 2 Tbsp. of heavy whipping cream
- Dash of salt
- ½ cup of espresso, freshly brewed
- 4 Tbsp. of powdered cocoa, unsweetened

Directions:

1. Preheat the oven to 375 degrees. Line a cake pan with a sheet of parchment paper.

2. In a bowl, add in the egg whites. Beat with a mix until frothy in consistency. Add in ½ cup of white sugar. Continue to beat until peaks begin to form on the surface. Transfer into the fridge and chill until you are ready to use it.

3. In a separate bowl, add in the egg yolks, 2 tablespoons of water and remaining ½ cup of white sugar. Beat with a mix until fluffy in consistency. Add in the reserved meringue and fold gently to incorporate.

4. In a separate bowl, add in the white flour, cornstarch and dash of salt. Stir well to mix. Add in the egg yolk mixture and fold gently to mix. Pour into the cake pan.

5. Place into the oven to bake for 8 to 10 minutes or until golden. Remove and transfer onto a wire rack to cool completely.

6. Prepare the mascarpone cream. In a bowl, add in the mascarpone, white sugar, egg yolks, dark rum, heavy whipping cream and dash of salt. Beat with a mixer until peaks begin to form.

7. Pour the espresso over the baked cake.

8. Spread the mascarpone over the top and along the sides.

9. Sprinkle the cocoa over the top.

10. Serve immediately.

Chicken Piccata Pasta

If you love chicken piccata, then you need to try this pasta dish which brings a whole new flavor to a classic Italian dish.

Makes: 4 servings

Total Prep Time: 20 minutes

Ingredients:

- 2 chicken breasts, boneless, skinless and cut into pieces
- Dash of salt and black pepper
- ½ cup of white flour
- Extra virgin olive oil, as needed
- 2 Tbsp. of butter, soft
- 2 cloves of garlic, minced
- ¼ cup of dried white wine
- ½ cup of chicken stock
- ¼ cup heavy whipping cream
- 1 lemon, juice only
- ¼ cup of capers, drained
- 8 ounces of angel hair pasta, cooked
- ½ cup of parmesan cheese, grated
- 2 Tbsp. of flat leaf parsley, chopped

Directions:

1. Season the chicken with a dash of salt and black pepper. Dredge the chicken pieces in the white flour.

2. In a skillet set over medium to high heat. Add in 1 tablespoon of olive oil. Add in the coated chicken pieces. Cook for 8 to 10 minutes or until browned. Transfer the chicken onto a plate and set aside. Wipe the skillet clean with a few paper towels.

3. Lower the heat to low. Add in the butter and minced garlic. Cook for 1 minute or until fragrant.

4. Add in the dried white wine and allow to come to a simmer. Cook for 1 minute. Add in the chicken stock, lemon juice and drained capers. Stir well to mix and allow to come to a simmer. Deglaze the bottom of the skillet.

5. Add in the heavy whipping cream.

6. Add the cooked chicken and cooked angel hair pasta. Add in the grated Parmesan cheese. Toss until coated.

7. Remove from heat. Serve with a topping of the chopped parsley.

Cheesy Italian Chicken

This is a delicious and easy Italian dish you can make any night of the week. It is packed with a flavor that you won't be able to resist.

Makes: 4 servings

Total Prep Time: 30 minutes

Ingredients:

- 4 chicken breasts, boneless and skinless
- Dash of salt and black pepper
- 3 Tbsp. of extra virgin olive oil, evenly divided
- ½ cup of pesto
- 1 tomato, thinly sliced
- 4 slices of mozzarella cheese
- 4 basil leaves
- ¾ pound of spaghetti, cooked
- 1 lemon, juice only
- ½ cup of Parmesan cheese, grated

Directions:

1. In a skillet set over medium to high heat, add in 1 tablespoon of olive oil.

2. Season the chicken breasts with a dash of salt and black pepper. Place into the skillet. Cook for 5 minutes on each side or until seared.

3. Spoon 2 tablespoons of the pesto over the chicken. Continue to cook for an additional 4 minutes on each side.

4. Top off with the slices of mozzarella cheese and slices of tomato. Cover and cook for 5 minutes.

5. In a separate skillet, add the cooked spaghetti, lemon juice, remaining olive oil and grated Parmesan cheese. Season with a dash of salt and black pepper. Toss well to coat.

6. Serve the chicken breasts on top of the pasta. Season with a dash of salt and black pepper. Garnish with the basil leaves.

Cherry and Pistachio Biscotti

This is a classic Italian snack that you can make whenever you are craving something simple to snack on. Perfect for those on a diet.

Makes: 48 servings

Total Prep Time: 1 hour and 30 minutes

Ingredients:

- 1 ¾ cup of white flour
- 1 cup of white sugar
- ½ cup of old fashioned oats
- 1 tsp. of baker's style baking powder
- ½ tsp. of baker's style baking soda
- ½ tsp. of salt
- 2 eggs
- 3 Tbsp. of vegetable oil
- 1 Tbsp. of orange zest
- 1 ½ tsp. of pure vanilla
- ½ tsp. of almond extract
- 1 cup of dried cherries
- 1 cup of pistachios, shelled

Directions:

1. Heat up the oven to 350 degrees. Place a sheet of parchment paper onto a baking sheet.

2. In a bowl of a stand mixer, add in the white flour, white sugar, old fashioned oats, dash of salt, baker's style baking powder and soda. Mix well until evenly mixed.

3. In a separate bowl, add in the eggs, vegetable oil, orange zest, pure vanilla, pistachios, cherries and almond extra. Beat until evenly mixed.

4. Transfer the dough onto a flat surface. Divide in half. Shape each piece into a 16 inch log. Place onto the baking sheet.

5. Place into the oven to bake for 30 minutes or until set. Remove and place on a wire rack to cool for 15 minutes.

6. Reduce the temperature of the oven to 250 degrees.

7. Line another baking sheet with a sheet of parchment paper. Transfer the bicotti onto a flat surface. Slice into 2/3 inch sized slices and place with the cut side down onto the baking sheet.

8. Place into the oven to bake for 40 minutes or until crispy. Remove and transfer onto a wire rack to cool before serving.

Classic Spaghetti and Meatballs

This is a classic Italian dish that the entire family won't be able to get enough of. It is the perfect dish to make any night of the week.

Makes: 4 servings

Total Prep Time: 1 hour

Ingredients:

- 1 pound of ground beef
- 1/3 cup of breadcrumbs
- 1/4 cup of parsley, chopped
- ¼ cup of parmesan cheese, grated
- 1 egg
- 2 cloves of garlic, minced
- 1 tsp. of salt
- ½ tsp. of crushed red pepper flakes
- 2 Tbsp. of extra virgin olive oil, evenly divided
- ½ cup of onion, chopped
- 1 bay leaf
- 1, 35 ounce can of tomatoes, crushed
- Dash of salt and black pepper
- 1 pound of spaghetti, cooked

Directions:

1. In a bowl, add in the ground beef, breadcrumbs, chopped parsley, egg, grated parmesan cheese, egg, minced garlic and crushed red pepper flakes. Season with a dash of salt and black pepper. Stir well to mix.

2. Shape the mix into 16 balls.

3. In a pot set over medium to high heat, add in 1 tablespoon of olive oil. Add in the meatballs and cook for 10 minutes or until cooked through. Remove and set aside on a plate to cool.

4. Add in the remaining olive oil. Add in the onion. Cook for 5 minutes or until translucent.

5. Add in the bay leaf and can of crushed tomatoes. Season with a dash of salt and black pepper. Allow to come to a simmer.

6. Add the cooked meatballs. Cover and continue to cook for 8 to 10 minutes. Remove from heat.

7. Serve the meatballs over the cooked spaghetti and the sauce poured over the top. Garnish with Parmesan cheese.

Classic Chicken Florentine

One bite of this classic Italian dish and it will soon become your new favorite Italian meal. Serve with fresh Italian bread for the tastiest results.

Makes: 4 servings

Total Prep Time: 45 minutes

Ingredients:

- 12 ounces of penne
- 1 Tbsp. of extra virgin olive oil
- 1 pound of chicken breasts, boneless and skinless
- Dash of salt and black pepper
- ½ tsp. of oregano
- 1/3 cup of dried white wine
- 2 cloves of garlic, minced
- 1 ½ cup of tomato, chopped
- 1 cup of heavy whipping cream
- 1 cup of mozzarella cheese, shredded
- ½ cup of parmesan cheese, grated and extra for serving
- 1 ½ cup of baby spinach
- 2 Tbsp. of parsley, chopped
- Red pepper flakes, optional and for garnish

Directions:

1. In a pot set over medium to high heat, fill with salted water. Add in the penne pasta and cook for 10 to 12 minutes or until soft. Drain and set the pasta aside.

2. In a skillet set over medium to high heat, add in 1 tablespoon of olive oil. Season the chicken breasts with a dash of salt, black pepper and oregano. Add into the skillet and cook for 8 to 10 minutes or until browned. Transfer to a flat surface and set aside to rest for 5 minutes. Slice into strips.

3. Prepare the sauce. In the skillet, pour in the dried white wine. Deglaze the bottom of the skillet. Allow to come to a simmer.

4. Add in the chopped tomato and minced garlic. Cook for 2 minutes.

5. Add in the heavy whipping cream and allow to come back to a simmer. Add in the shredded mozzarella cheese and grated parmesan cheese. Cook for 1 to 2 minutes or until the cheese has melted. Season with a dash of salt and black pepper.

6. Remove the skillet from heat. Add in the cooked penne pasta, baby spinach, chopped parsley and red pepper flakes. Stir well until coated in the sauce.

7. Serve immediately.

Skillet Pizza Primavera

If you love the taste of pizza, then this is a dish you need to try for yourself. It is made using fresh Italian ingredients, you will never want to order boring takeout pizza ever again.

Makes: 2 servings

Total Prep Time: 45 minutes

Ingredients:

- 2 red bell peppers, thinly sliced
- ½ of a head of broccoli, chopped into florets
- ¼ of a red onion, thinly sliced
- 1 cup of cherry tomatoes, chopped into halves
- Extra virgin olive oil, as needed
- Dash of salt and black pepper
- White flour, for dusting
- 1 pound of pizza dough
- 1 cup of ricotta cheese
- 1 cup of mozzarella cheese, shredded

Directions:

1. Preheat the oven to 400 degrees.

2. On a baking sheet, add the sliced red bell peppers, broccoli florets, sliced red onion and cherry tomato halves. Pour 1 to 2 tablespoons of olive oil over the mix. Season with a dash of salt and black pepper. Toss well until mixed.

3. Place into the oven to bake for 18 to 20 minutes. Remove.

4. Increase the temperature of the oven to 500 degrees.

5. Grease a cast iron skillet with oil.

6. On a floured surface, roll out the pizza dough until it fits into the inside of the cast iron skillet. Transfer into the skillet and grease the dough with olive oil.

7. Add dollops of the ricotta cheese over the dough. Sprinkle the shredded mozzarella cheese over the top. Top off with the baked veggies. Drizzle 1 tablespoon of olive oil over the top and season with a dash of salt.

8. Place into the oven to bake for 12 minutes.

9. Remove and serve immediately.

Tomato Bruschetta

This is a hearty and delicious Italian dish you can make whenever you want to spoil your significant other with something special. It makes for the perfect appetizer to serve before an authentic Italian meal.

Makes: 12 servings

Total Prep Time: 35 minutes

Ingredients:

- 6 roma tomatoes, chopped
- ½ cup of sundried tomatoes, packed in oil
- 3 cloves of garlic, minced
- ¼ cup of extra virgin olive oil
- 2 Tbsp. of balsamic vinegar
- ¼ cup of basil, chopped
- ¼ tsp. of salt
- ¼ tsp. of black pepper
- 1 French baguette
- 2 cups of mozzarella cheese, shredded

Directions:

1. Preheat the oven to broil.

2. In a bowl, add in the roma and sundried tomatoes, minced garlic, oil, vinegar and chopped basil. Season with a dash of salt and black pepper. Stir well to mix. Set aside to rest for 10 minutes.

3. Slice the baguette into ¾ inch thick slices. Place onto a baking sheet.

4. Place into the oven to broil for 1 to 2 minutes or until light brown.

5. Top the bread slices with the tomato mix. Sprinkle the shredded mozzarella cheese over the top.

6. Place back into the oven to broil for 5 minutes.

7. Remove and serve immediately.

Italian Mac and Cheese

This is the perfect Italian dish to serve to the picky eaters in your household. After taking a few bites, I guarantee they will be asking for seconds.

Makes: 6 servings

Total Prep Time: 1 hour

Ingredients:

- Dash of salt and black pepper
- 1 pound of cavatappi
- ½ cup of butter, soft
- 2 cloves of garlic, minced
- ½ cup of white flour
- 5 cups of whole milk
- ½ tsp. of Italian seasoning
- Dash of red pepper flakes
- 4 cups of mozzarella cheese, shredded
- 1 cup of grated parmesan cheese
- 4 tomatoes, thinly sliced
- 2 Tbsp. of basil, thinly sliced
- ¼ cup of Italian breadcrumbs
- Balsamic glaze, for drizzling

Directions:

1. Preheat the oven to 375 degrees. Grease a baking dish with butter.

2. In a pot set over medium to high heat, fill with salted water. Add in the cavatappi pasta. Cook for 10 minutes or until soft. Drain the set the pasta aside.

3. In a saucepan set over medium to high heat, add in 1 stick of butter. Add in the minced garlic and white flour. Whisk to mix. Cook for 1 to 2 minutes or until gold.

4. Add in the whole milk and whisk until smooth in consistency. Season with the Italian seasoning, red pepper flakes, dash of salt and dash of black pepper. Simmer for 5 minutes or until thick in consistency.

5. Remove from heat. Add in the mozzarella cheese and 1 cup of parmesan cheese. Whisk until smooth in consistency. Add in the cooked pasta and toss well to mix.

6. Transfer into the baking dish.

7. Sprinkle the Italian breadcrumbs over the top. Add the tomato slices. Season with a dash of salt and black pepper.

8. Place into the oven to bake for 25 to 30 minutes.

9. Remove and garnish with the chopped basil and a drizzling of the balsamic glaze.

Italian Tortellini Soup

This is the perfect soup dish for you to make whenever you need something to warm you up on a cold winter's night.

Makes: 4 servings

Total Prep Time: 30 minutes

Ingredients:

- 1 Tbsp. of extra virgin olive oil
- 1 yellow onion, chopped
- 1 pound of chicken sausage
- 4 cloves of garlic, minced
- 1, 28 ounce can of tomatoes, crushed
- 4 cups of low sodium chicken broth
- 1 tsp. of crushed red pepper flakes
- Dash of salt and black pepper
- 2, 9 ounce packs of cheese tortellini
- 1, 15 ounce can of white beans, drained
- 5 ounces of baby spinach
- Parmesan cheese, grated and for garnish

Directions:

1. In a pot set over medium to high heat, add in the olive oil. Add in the chopped yellow onion. Cook for 5 minutes or until gold.

2. Add in the chicken sausage. Cook for 5 minutes or until gold.

3. Add in the minced garlic, can of crushed tomatoes, low sodium chicken broth and crushed red pepper flakes. Season with a dash of salt and black pepper. Stir well to mix.

4. Allow to come to a simmer. Cook for 5 minutes.

5. Add in the drained white beans and baby spinach. Stir well to mix. Cook for 1 minute or until wilted.

6. Remove from heat. Serve with a garnish of grated Parmesan cheese.

Lemon Carbonara Bucatini

This is an Italian dish that is packed with a savory lemon flavor that I know you will love. Once you try it, you will never go back to any other cuisine ever again.

Makes: 4 servings

Total Prep Time: 30 minutes

Ingredients:

- 1 Tbsp. of extra virgin olive oil
- 6 ounces of pancetta, thinly sliced
- 2 shallots, chopped
- 4 cloves of garlic, thinly sliced
- 1 tsp. of black pepper
- 12 ounces of bucatini
- Dash of salt
- 2 ounces of grated Parmesan cheese, extra for serving
- 2 egg yolks
- 1 tsp. of lemon zest, grated and extra for serving
- 2 Tbsp. of lemon juice

Directions:

1. In a skillet set over medium to high heat, add in the olive oil. Add in the sliced pancetta. Cook for 6 to 8 minutes or until crispy.

2. Add in the chopped shallots and sliced garlic. Stir well to mix. Cook for 5 minutes or until soft.

3. Add in the black pepper and continue to cook for an additional minute.

4. In a pot set over medium to high heat, fill with salted water. Allow to come to a boil. Add in the bucatini pasta. Cook for 8 to 10 minutes or until soft. Drain and set aside. Make sure to reserve 1 ½ cups of the pasta cooking liquid.

5. Transfer the pasta and ½ cup of the pasta liquid into the skillet. Add in 1 ounce of the parmesan cheese and toss well to coat. Remove from heat.

6. Add in the egg yolks and toss again. Add in the remaining pasta liquid.

7. Add in the lemon zest, lemon juice and remaining Parmesan cheese. Toss well to coat.

8. Serve immediately.

Gricia Pasta

This is another classic Italian pasta dish you can make whenever you are craving homemade pasta. Made with a salty and wholesome taste, everyone who tries this dish will love it.

Makes: 2 servings

Total Prep Time: 35 minutes

Ingredients:

- 1 Tbsp. of extra virgin olive oil
- 6 ounces of guanciale, cut into pieces
- 8 ounces of rigatoni pasta
- Dash of salt
- 2 tsp. of black pepper
- 3 ounces of Pecorino Romano, grated

Directions:

1. In a skillet set over low to medium heat, add in the olive oil. Add in the guanciale. Cook for 10 to 15 minutes or until crispy. Transfer into a bowl and set aside.

2. In a pot set over medium to high heat, fill with salted water. Allow to come to a boil. Add in the rigatoni pasta. Cook for 8 to 10 minutes or until soft. Drain and set aside. Make sure to reserve 1 ½ cups of the pasta liquid.

3. In the skillet, add in ¾ cup of the reserved pasta liquid. Allow to come to a boil and deglaze the bottom of the skillet.

4. Add the cooked pasta into the skillet. Continue to cook for 5 to 8 minutes or until a thick sauce begins to form.

5. Increase the temperature to medium or high. Add in the cooked guanciale, black pepper and grated Pecorino Romano cheese. Toss well to mix.

6. Remove from heat. Serve with a topping of grated Pecorino romano cheese.

Classic Fettucine Alfredo

You can't have an Italian cookbook without a fettucine alfredo recipe. This fettucine alfredo recipe is so delicious, it will rival those made by your favorite Italian restaurants.

Makes: 4 servings

Total Prep Time: 20 minutes

Ingredients:

- 12 ounces of fettuccine
- Dash of salt
- ¼ cup of butter, soft
- ¾ cup of Parmesan cheese, grated and extra for serving
- Dash of black pepper

Directions:

1. Prepare the pasta. In a pot set over medium to high heat, fill with salted water. Allow to come to a boil. Add in the fettuccine. Cook for 8 to 10 minutes or until soft. Drain and set aside. Make sure to reserve 2 cups of the pasta liquid.

2. Pour 1 cup of the pasta liquid into a skillet set over medium heat. Allow to come to a simmer.

3. Add in the butter and whisk until melted.

4. Add in the grated Parmesan cheese and whisk until mixed.

5. Add in the cooked fettuccine. Toss well until coated.

6. Add in more pasta liquid until the sauce is to the desired consistency. Remove from heat.

7. Serve with a topping of black pepper and grated Parmesan cheese.

Stuffed Italian Shells with Marinara Sauce

If you need an Italian dish that will impress your friends and family, then this is the perfect dish for you to make. Make this for your next special occasion.

Makes: 8 servings

Total Prep Time: 1 hour and 10 minutes

Ingredients:

- 12 ounces of jumbo pasta shells
- Dash of salt
- 2 egg yolks
- 1 egg
- 2 cups of whole ricotta cheese
- 3 ounces of Parmesan cheese, grated and extra for serving
- ¼ cup of parsley, chopped
- 8 ounces of mozzarella cheese, grated and evenly divided
- Dash of black pepper
- 3 cups of marinara sauce, evenly divided
- Dried oregano, for serving
- Extra virgin olive oil, for serving

Directions:

1. Preheat the oven to 375 degrees.

2. In a pot set over medium to high heat, fill with salted water. Allow to come to a boil. Add in the jumbo pasta shells. Cook for 10 to 15 minutes or until soft. Drain the pasta shells and set aside.

3. In a bowl, add in the egg yolks and egg. Whisk well until lightly beaten. Add in the whole ricotta cheese, grated Parmesan cheese, chopped parsley and 1 ½ cups of mozzarella cheese. Season with a dash of salt and black pepper. Stir well until evenly mixed. Transfer this mix into a Ziploc bag.

4. Spread 1 ½ cups of the marinara sauce into a baking dish.

5. Slice the corner of the Ziploc bag and pipe the filling into the cooked pasta shells. Place the shells into the baking dish. Pour 1 ½ cups of the marinara sauce and remaining mozzarella cheese over the shells.

6. Cover with a sheet of aluminum foil and place into the oven to bake for 35 to 40 minutes. Remove and set aside to rest for 5 minutes.

7. Increase the temperature of the oven to broil. Remove the sheet of aluminum foil and broil for 2 minutes or until browned on the top. Remove.

8. Serve immediately with a garnish of dried oregano, Parmesan cheese and a drizzling of olive oil.

Steak Pizzaiola

If you never thought that Italian cuisine can be made up of steak, then you will be pleasantly surprised once you try this dish for yourself.

Makes: 4 servings

Total Prep Time: 15 minutes

Ingredients:

- 2, ½ inch rib eye steaks, boneless
- Dash of salt and black pepper
- 2 Tbsp. of extra virgin olive oil, for serving
- 2 cloves of garlic, thinly sliced
- 1 sprig of basil
- Dash of crushed red pepper flakes
- 1 cup of marinara sauce
- Dried oregano, for serving

Directions:

1. Season the steaks with a dash of salt and black pepper.

2. In a skillet set over medium to high heat, add in 2 tablespoons of olive oil. Add in the steaks. Cook for 5 minutes or until browned. Drain the excess grease and set aside to rest.

3. Add in the garlic into the skillet. Cook for 30 seconds.

4. Add in the basil sprig and crushed red pepper flakes. Stir well to mix. Add in the marinara sauce and allow to come to a simmer.

5. Add in the cooked steaks and spoon the sauce over the steaks to cover. Continue to cook for 3 minutes.

6. Transfer the steaks to a plate. Serve with the oregano over the top.

Mortadella Beef Meatballs

If you love the taste of classic Italian meatballs, then this is one dish I know you will fall in love with. Smothered in plenty of marinara sauce, these meatballs are incredibly tender and easy to make.

Makes: 4 servings

Total Prep Time: 1 hour and 15 minutes

Ingredients:

- ¼ cup of extra virgin olive oil
- 1 onion, chopped
- 1 carrot, chopped
- 1 stalk of celery, chopped
- ½ cup of tomato paste
- 1, 28 ounce can of tomatoes, crushed
- 1 cup of heavy whipping cream
- 1 tsp. of salt
- Dash of black pepper
- 1 pound of ground beef
- ½ pound of mortadella, cut into small pieces
- 2 eggs
- 1/3 cup of fine breadcrumbs
- ¼ cup of parsley, chopped
- 2 Tbsp. of oregano, chopped
- Pecorino Romano cheese, grated and for serving

Directions:

1. In a pot set over medium to high heat, add in the olive oil. Add in the chopped onion, chopped carrot and chopped celery. Season with a dash of salt and black pepper. Stir well to mix. Cook for 10 to 15 minutes or until soft.

2. Add in the tomato paste and continue to cook for 5 minutes or until dark.

3. Add in the crushed can of tomatoes and heavy whipping cream. Stir well to mix and allow to come to a boil. Lower the heat to low. Season with a dash of salt and black pepper. Allow to come to a simmer.

4. In a bowl, add in the ground beef, mortadella, eggs, fine breadcrumbs, chopped parsley, dried oregano and dash of salt. Stir well with your hands until evenly mixed. Form into balls that are 1 ½ inches in diameter.

5. Transfer the meatballs into the pot. Cover and cook for 40 to 45 minutes or until cooked through. Remove from heat.

6. Serve immediately with a topping of the grated Pecorino Romano cheese.

Seared Steak Tartare

This is another delicious steak dish I know you will want to make as often as possible. Serve with a salad for the tastiest results.

Makes: 1 serving

Total Prep Time: 10 minutes

Ingredients:

- 1, 8 ounce New York strip steak, boneless
- 1 Tbsp. of extra virgin olive oil, extra for drizzling
- Dash of salt and black pepper
- 1 sprig of rosemary
- 2 cloves of garlic, unpeeled
- Dash of sea salt

Directions:

1. Chop the steak into ¼ inch sized pieces. Place into a bowl. Season with a dash of salt and black pepper.

2. In a skillet set over medium to high heat, add in the steak pieces. Coo for 3 to 5 minutes or until browned. Remove and transfer onto a plate.

3. In the same skillet, add in the sprig of rosemary and unpeeled garlic cloves. Stir well to mix. Cook for 3 minutes or until browned.

4. Top the steaks with the garlic mix. Season with a dash of sea salt and serve immediately.

Conclusion

Well, there you have it!

Hopefully by the end of this Italian cookbook you have learned not only how to make some of the most authentic Italian recipes completely from scratch, but have learned a thing or two about Italian cooking in the process. Hopefully, by the end of this book not only have you discovered over 25 different Italian recipes that you can make from the comfort of your own home, but feel confident in preparing authentic Italian dishes.

So, what is next for you?

The next step for you to take is to begin making some of these delicious Italian dishes for yourself. Once you have done that, it will be time for you to try your hand at making your own Italian recipes from scratch.

Good luck!

Author's Afterthoughts

Thanks Ever So Much to Each of My Cherished Readers for Investing the Time to Read This Book!

I know you could have picked from many other books but you chose this one. So, big thanks for buying this book and reading all the way to the end.

If you enjoyed this book or received value from it, I'd like to ask you for a favor. Please take a few minutes to post an honest and heartfelt review on **Amazon.** Your support does make a difference and helps to benefit other people.

Thank you!

Carla Hale

About the Author

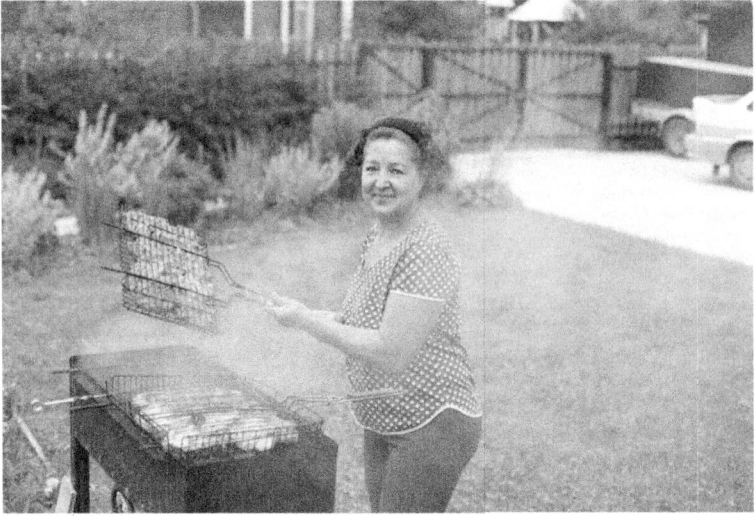

Carla Hale

I think of myself as a foodie. I like to eat, yes. I like to cook even more. I like to prepare meals for my family and friends, I feel like that's what I was born to do...

My name is Carla Hale and as may have suspected already, I am originally from Scotland. I am first and foremost a mother, a wife, but simultaneously over the years I became a proclaimed cook. I have shared my recipes with many and will continue to do so, as long as I can. I like different. I dress different, I love different, I speak different and I cook different. I like to think that I am different because I am more animated about what I do than most; I feel more and care more.

It served me right when cooking to sprinkle some tenderness, love, passion, in every dish I prepare. It does not matter if I am preparing a meal for strangers passing by my cooking booth at the flea market or if I am making my mother's favorite recipe. Each and every meal I prepare from scratch will contain a little bite of my life story and little part of my heart in it. People feel it, taste it and ask for more! Thank you for taking the time to get to know me and hopefully through my recipes you can learn a lot more about my influences and preferences. Who knows you might just find your own favorite within my repertoire! Enjoy!

Printed in Great Britain
by Amazon

25979675R00051